Dennis the Menace

and his

By HANK KETCHAM

FAWCETT GOLD MEDAL • NEW YORK

A Fawcett Gold Medal Book

Published by Ballantine Books

Copyright © 1974, 1975 by The Hill Syndicate, Inc.

Copyright © 1977 by CBS Publications, The Consumer Publishing Division of CBS, Inc.

ISBN 0-449-12791-5

This edition published by arrangement with
The Hall Syndicate

Printed in Canada

First Fawcett Gold Medal Edition: May 1977
First Ballantine Books Edition: August 1984

"RUFF WANTS TO PLAY DOLLS WITH YA, MARGARET. JUST THROW IT AS FAR AS YOU CAN!"

"TWINKLE, TWINKLE,
LITTLE STAR...."

"SHE TALKS TO BIRDS, TREES,
FLOWERS...*ANYTHING.*"

"NOW *THAT'S* WHAT I CALL A *DANCE!*"

" ICE CUBE."

"GIRLS CAN PLAY BASEBALL AND CLIMB TREES AND..."

"YOU CAN KILL A WHOLE DAY JUST *LISTENIN'* TO HER."

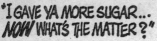

"I GAVE YA MORE SUGAR...
NOW WHAT'S THE MATTER?"

"*BOY!* LOOK AT HIM *GO!*"

"GOSH, GINA...YOU REMIND ME A LOT OF MY *MOM*."

"BUT I'M *NOT* YOUR MOM... AND DON' YOU FORGET IT!"

"MARGARET SAYS YOU'RE *EARTHY*... WHAT DOES THAT MEAN?"

"THAT MEANS SOME OF US GOTS IT, AND SOME HASN'T."

"YOU AN' ME GET ALONG REAL GOOD, GINA...TOO BAD YOU'RE A GIRL."

"YOU THINK SO, HUH?"

"...AN' YOU MIGHT AS WELL BLESS MARGARET AND THAT FRESH KID DOWN THE BLOCK, IF YOU'RE NOT TOO BUSY."

"FUNERAL'S OFF...MY MOM TOOK CHARGE OF THE MOUSE."

"NOT YET. HE LIKES TO RELAX WHEN HE GETS HOME FROM THE OFFICE. I'LL TELL HIM LATER."

"YOU HEARD HIM, HENRY...JUST PUNCH THE *IDIOT* BUTTON."

" I JUST THOUGHT OF SOMETHIN' WE CAN
TALK ABOUT...TAKIN' A *BATH* IN *ICE CREAM!*"

"HE SAYS IT MEANS *TOUGH LUCK, KID.*"

"IT'S A *DULL PICKLE*...I'M STILL DECIDIN' WHETHER I LIKE IT OR NOT."

"IS THAT SOMETHIN' I COULD SAY IF I EVER GO TO ITALY?"

"DON' YOU DARE!"

"YOU'RE A GOOD-LOOKIN'
KID... SO FAR."

"TALK *NICE* AN' CARRY
A *UMBRELLA*."

"THERE'S SOMETHIN' ABOUT GINA I CAN'T FIGGER OUT."

"WAIT."

"GINA MEANS SHE HAD SIX *PIGLETS* THAT FOLLOWED HER EVERYWHERE."

"I LIKE *PYGMIES* BETTER."

"ONE GOOD THING ABOUT OL' MARGARET...SHE'S TOO *SANITARY* TO WANT A LICK OF ANYONE ELSE'S CONE."

"I'M THROUGH. WHILE YOU'RE FINISHING, I'M GONNA TAKE UP A BONE COLLECTION FOR RUFF."

"CREAMED TUNA... SHE FORGOT TO TAKE
THE MEAT OUT OF THE FREEZER AGAIN."

"DON'T SHOOT HIM! HE WAS AIMIN' AT ME!"

"IT'S TOO *HOT* T'SLEEP!"

"YA WANNA KNOW SOMETHIN'?
CLEAN ROOMS ARE *BORING!*"

"YEAH, BUT WHERE DO YA PLUG IT IN?"

"WHAT DID YA DO WITH ALL YOUR SPARE TIME BEFORE I WAS BORN, MOM?"

"WE MIGHT AS WELL GET OUT...THAT'S ALL THE WARNING
HE GIVES BEFORE HE GETS *IN*."

"YOUR MOTHER WANTS YOU, DENNIS."

"WHY ELSE WOULD SHE HAVE *HAD* HIM?"

"NOW LOOK WHAT YOU'VE DONE! I HAD THAT TRAP ALL SET FOR THE *TOOTH FAIRY!*"

"ANOTHER GOOD THING ABOUT PEANUT BUTTER...THE JAR MAY *LOOK* EMPTY, BUT YOU CAN _ALWAYS_ GET SOME MORE OUT OF IT !"

"I ALREADY TOOK 'EM OFF AT MR. WILSON'S. THESE ARE MY *FEET!*"

"IS THIS ANY WAY TO TREAT
THE ONLY KID YA GOT?"

"DAD'S SMILIN'. HE MUSTA HAD A SOFT DAY AT THE OFFICE."

"MY FOLKS ARE THE SAME WAY... WHEN THEY START REALLY *HOWLIN'* ABOUT SOMETHING, YA MIGHT AS WELL GIVE UP."

"CROSS MY HEART AN' HOPE TO EAT MY WEIGHT IN CARROTS."

"IT SAYS HERE THAT YOU CAN TURN *ORANGE* FROM EATING TOO MANY CARROTS."

"*AHA!*"

"YOU'LL HAVTA TALK *LOUDER*, JOEY...THERE'S A LOTA *SMOOCHIN'* AND *GIGGLIN'* GOIN' ON HERE!"

"I'LL CERTAINLY SPEAK TO HIM ABOUT IT."

"YA CALL *THAT* SPEAKIN'?"

"I CAN'T SETTLE DOWN TO WORK YET. GUESS I'M STILL TOO FULL OF SUMMER."

"SHE'S GOT A *BROTHER*... WOULD IT BE OKAY TO BEAT *HIM* UP?"

"OKAY..THAT'S THREE BALONEY AN' FOUR PEANUT BUTTER SAMWICHES."

"MY MOM SAYS THE REST'RUNT IS *CLOSED!*"

"AWWWW... I THOUGHT IT WAS A BAD WORD."

"MR. WILSON TOLD ME TO *SKEEDADDLE.*
HOW DO YA DO THAT ?"

"THAT'S A PIECE OF MY
WEDDING CAKE."

"NO *WONDER* YA DIDN'T
EAT IT!"

"THIS IS MY WEDDING PICTURE."

"IS THIS SKINNY GUY YOUR *FIRST* HUSBAND?"

"THIS WAS TAKEN WHEN GEORGE AND I WERE COURTING."

"WHATEVER BECAME OF THE *HORSE*?"

"YOU MEAN *BOTH* OF YOU...IN THE SAME CANOE?"

"MY FATHER WAS A STERN-LOOKING MAN, DENNIS."

"YOU SHOULD HAVE SEEN HIM *SMILE* AT THE WEDDING."

"DON'T BE IN A HURRY TO GROW UP, JOEY...
IT'S NOT THAT BIG A DEAL."

"I COULDN'T SELL THESE WORMS I DUG UP YESTERDAY, SO I BROUGHT 'EM *BACK*."

"THAT'S *SILLY*...HOW COULD THERE BE TOO MUCH SUGAR IN IT?"

"YEAH, SHE DOES NICE WORK...BUT YA GOTTA HANDLE HER *JUST SO.*"

"SHE DIDN'T SIT *ME* ... SHE SAT THE *PHONE!*"

"DEWEY DON'T HAVE TO WEAR IT NO MORE, SO HE GAVE IT TO *ME*."

"MADEMOISELLE FROM ARMENTIERS, PARLEY VOO...♪"

"HOW COME YOU'RE *HUMMIN'* PART OF THE WORDS?"

"THAT'S ADDING *INSULT* TO *INJURY* !"

" YOU MEAN LIKE *CREAMED CARROTS* ?"

"WANNA HEAR A GOOD ONE ON OL' MARGARET?
DEWEY SAYS SHE'S BEEN TAKIN' *UGLY* LESSONS."

"*YOU* DON'T HAVE TO DO THAT, MR. WILSON...
I'LL TOUCH 'EM FOR YA!"

"SORRY, DEWEY... SATURDAY IS THE DAY MY
DAD NEEDS ME TO BE A PAL TO HIM."

"JUST BECAUSE YOU WOKE UP FIRST FOR A CHANGE, IT DON'T MEAN I'M *SICK!*"

"GOOD HEAVENS! ... WHAT WAS *THAT* ?"

"NEXT TIME YOU GO TO THE FIXIT SHOP, I GOT SOMETHIN' FOR YOU."

"DON'T TELL ME HE'S
SAYING *GRACE!*"

"LOOKING FOR *CARROTS.*"

"GEE WHIZ...DO I TELL *YOU* YOU'RE GETTIN' HEAVY?"

"NO, THERE AREN'T ANY TEEN-AGERS IN THIS NEIGHBORHOOD,
BUT THERE'S A *PARENT-AGER* NEXT DOOR."

"MARGARET SWALLOWED A WHAT?"

"A DICTIONARY."

"CHOCOLATE-COVERED CARROTS? YA *WOULDN'T!*"

"*WHEW!* THAT STUFF SMELLED PRETTY GOOD UNTIL YA SET FIRE TO IT."

"IT'S NO FUN PLAYIN' HIDE-AN'-SEEK WITH MR. WILSON. HE DON'T EVEN *TRY* TO FIND ME!"

"I SPENT ALL *SUMMER* COLLECTIN' THOSE BUGS, AN'
IN TWO SECONDS... *WHOOSH!*"

"HE DIDN'T EXACTLY *BITE* ME...HE JUST STARTED EATIN' SOMETHING BEFORE I COULD LET GO OF IT."

"MOM! HOW DO YA GET KETCHUP OUT OF THIS BOTTLE?"

"NEVER MIND...I GOT IT. *DON'T COME IN HERE!*"

"I'M NOT EXACTLY *SICK*...BUT MY STOMACH IS THINKIN' IT OVER."

"...AND CLEAN UP THIS MESS!"

"CAN'TCHA TAKE A JOKE?"

"OUCH! YOUR FACE NEEDS A *HAIRCUT!*"

"WHEN I GROW UP I WANTA BE JUST LIKE *YOU*, MR. WILSON."

"RETIRED."

"THAT WAS THE EASY PART, JOEY. NOW THE TRICK IS GETTIN' IT BACK *IN!*"

"NOW THAT WE GOT TO HALLOWEEN, JOEY, IT'S *ALL DOWNHILL* TO CHRISTMAS!"

"YOU'RE JUST WASTIN' YOUR MONEY BUYIN' A *MASK*, MARGARET."

"MEASLES...NOT *MEASLIES*."

"GINA OUGHTA KNOW...SHE'S
THE ONE THAT'S *GOT* 'EM."

"TAKE YOUR TIME, MOM. I'LL JUST
BE SMELLING AROUND."

"I BET WE COULD TRADE OUR HOUSE FOR A RANCH AN' OUR WASHING MACHINE FOR A HORSE...AN' THAT VACUUM CLEANER FOR A SADDLE..."

"I HOPE YOUR RAT WINS THE RACE, DAD!"

"WE DON'T *EAT* IN THE LIBRARY, DENNIS."

"HOW DO YA *LIVE* ?"

"WANNA PET MY SPIDER?"

"YOU'RE ALWAYS TELLIN' ME TO BE *NICE* TO HER."

"HE'S *LITTLE*, AIN'T HE? AND HE *CREEPS*, DON'T HE? SO WHAT'S WRONG WITH CALLIN' HIM A LITTLE ....."

"I THOUGHT YOU SAID HE'D BE GOOFIN' OFF
AT THIS TIME OF DAY..."

"IT DIDN'T DO MY COLORED CRAYONS NO GOOD, EITHER, YA KNOW... HOW 'BOUT *THAT*?"

"YOU WEREN'T EVEN
THOUGHT OF YET."

"I BET I MADE UP
FOR IT *SINCE*."

"*FETCH*, RUFF!"

"NOT THE PAPER BOY...
THE *PAPER!*"

"MARGARET'S TELLIN' ME ALL ABOUT HER NEW HAIR-DO."

"THIS IS MY MOM."

"I GOT A *DOG*, TOO."

"IF I TAKE OFF MY SHIRT AND PANTS, CAN I HAVE A *CHILI-DOG*?"

"I LIKED 'EM FINE UNTIL YA
TOLD ME WHAT THEY *WAS*."

"SOUR MILK PANCAKES."

"*TYING* FLIES? AT MY HOUSE WE *SWAT* 'EM!"

"SAY SOMETHIN' TO ME IN ITALIAN, GINA. THAT REALLY *GETS* MARGARET!"

"WE GOT A LOT IN COMMON. I'M A ONLY KID AN' HE'S A ONLY DOG!"

"IF I TELL HIM WHAT I GOT PLANNED FOR TODAY, IT'LL BE A LOT EASIER TO TALK TO HIM TONIGHT."

"I THINK I NEED SOME *SECOND*-AID, TOO."

"MMMM! MOM, IF I EVER SAVE ENOUGH MONEY TO BUY A FIRST PRIZE... YOU'RE GONNA *GET* IT!"

"I *DID* SAVE ROOM FOR PUNKIN PIE...BUT I THINK SOME STUFFIN' MOVED *INTO* IT."

"I'M WITH DENNIS...LET'S STICK HIM IN THE FREEZER UNTIL *NEXT* THANKSGIVING."

"GOOD NEWS! RUFF GOT THE REST OF THE TURKEY!"

"I WANT MY *BATH!*"

"A WHOLE *BOTTLE* OF MARGARET'S PERFUME...THE STOPPER CAME OUT!"

"YOU HAVE TEN SECONDS TO COMPLAIN, MR. WILSON. THIS IS A RECORDING."

"YOU GOT GOLF CLUBS AN' FISHIN' TACKLE, A BOWLING BALL 'N SKIS...
AN' ALL I'M ASKIN' FOR IS *ONE HORSE!*"

"MOM WANTS TO TELL YA *IN HER OWN WAY* HOW SHE DENTED THE FENDER."

"EVER NOTICE HOW SHE CALLS YOU 'HONEY' WHEN *SHE DOES* SOMETHIN'... AND 'HENRY' WHEN *YOU* DO IT?"

"BOY, I HOPE THEIR BATHROOM IS NEAR THE FRONT DOOR!"

"THERE'S NO PLEASIN' SOME PEOPLE ... I GOT MY *HANDS* NICE AN' CLEAN...SO NOW SHE'S YELLIN' ABOUT THE *TOWEL!*"

"DID YA EVER NOTICE HOW TALKIN' TO GINA IS LIKE LISTENIN' TO *BAND MUSIC*?"

"WHEN YOU'RE CALLING ON SOME-ONE, WHAT'S THE NICEST WAY TO *LEAVE*?"

"JUST SAY '*GOOD-BYE*' AN' *GO!*"

"GEE WHIZ! YOU GO RIGHT UP LIKE A *SKYROCKET* SOMETIMES!"

"BUT I COME RIGHT DOWN AGAIN."

"I'D LIKE TO SEE
GINA HIT *ME!*"

"HANG IN THERE."

"GOSH, GINA... YOU SMELL BETTER'N A PLATEFUL OF PEANUT BUTTER SAMWICHES!"

"THE ULTIMATE COMPLIMENT."

"I'M JUST GETTIN' SOME SMALL CHANGE READY IN CASE THE TOOTH FAIRY HAS ONLY GOT A DOLLAR BILL."

"BOY, EVERBODY IS AWFUL QUIET
WHO ARE WE MAD AT TONIGHT?"

"THE FIRST COUPLA TIMES SHE CLEANED MY ROOM,
I THOUGHT I'D BEEN *ROBBED*.

"I DON'T ANTICIPATE ANY DIFFICULTY, MRS. MITCHELL."

"NOW... LET ME TRANSLATE THAT."

"WHICH DID YOU LIKE BEST...THE PLAYING OR THE SINGING?"

"THE COOKIES."

"DON'T TAKE IT PERSONAL...SHE ONLY THREW YA OUT BECAUSE YOU WAS WITH *ME*."

HERE COMES TROUBLE!!!
DENNIS THE MENACE!!!

- ☐ Dennis the Menace—
  ### DRIVING MOTHER UP THE WALL
  14134 $1.50
- ☐ Dennis the Menace—
  ### GOOD INTENSHUNS 14395 $1.50
- ☐ Dennis the Menace—
  ### HERE COMES TROUBLE 13634 $1.50
- ☐ Dennis the Menace—
  ### I DONE IT MY WAY 14095 $1.50
- ☐ Dennis the Menace—
  ### THE KID NEXT DOOR 13656 $1.50
- ☐ Dennis the Menace—
  ### NON-STOP NUISANCE 13737 $1.50
- ☐ Dennis the Menace—
  ### OL' DROOPY DRAWERS 14004 $1.50
- ☐ Dennis the Menace—
  ### ONE MORE TIME 14423 $1.50
- ☐ Dennis the Menace—
  ### STAYIN' ALIVE 14363 $1.50

Buy them at your local bookstore or use this handy coupon for ordering.

COLUMBIA BOOK SERVICE, CBS Inc.
32275 Mally Road, P.O. Box FB, Madison Heights, MI 48071

Please send me the books I have checked above. Orders for less than 5 books must include 75¢ for the first book and 25¢ for each additional book to cover postage and handling. Orders for 5 books or more postage is FREE. Send check or money order only. Allow 3-4 weeks for delivery.

Cost $_____	Name _____
Sales tax*_____	Address _____
Postage_____	City _____
Total $_____	State _____ Zip _____

*The government requires us to collect sales tax in all states except AK, DE, MT, NH and OR.

Prices and availability subject to change without notice.